Because They Lived;

"Memories & Stories of Amazing Kids Lost to Suicide"

As Told by the Moms They Left Behind

Volume 5

Compiled by *Melissa Bottorff-Arey*
"The Leftover Pieces;®" Podcast Host

Dedication

—————— ♥ ——————

As you read these words, my friend-in-grief, you become a significant part of this moment. The concept of legacy is profound. It empowers us to remember those we cherished, to unearth new facts about them, and to perpetuate their influence, even beyond life. Your role in preserving this legacy is particularly significant.

This book is first and foremost dedicated to all of *you*—the heroes who support us, love us, and remember our children as we do. You make our world brighter and lighter, and you have helped make this book possible. We are deeply grateful for your unwavering support, which sustains us.

Next, to G.R.—I am eternally grateful for your unwavering love and support, the purest I have ever known. You keep me afloat through the storms, maintaining hope and stability when I falter. I don't know how you manage it all with such grace, but I will forever appreciate your steadfastness. To my two other children, Lauren and Parker, and my wonderfully magnificent grandchildren: everything I do, is for you. My love for all of you knows no bounds.

To the 'Leftover Pieces' Community of bereaved mothers—especially those cherished friends with whom I've shared countless hours and look forward to sharing many more—you are my guiding stars amidst the turbulence. You inspire me, motivate me and provide the anchor I so desperately need. Thank you from the depths of my heart.

Sharon and Suzanne, our trio, may seem unlikely, yet our connection feels as natural as the air we breathe. We are indeed kindred spirits, brought together by our beloved sons in spirit. Our bond transcends this world, intertwining us through shared tragedy and mutual healing.

And ultimately, this book is dedicated to our sons--Luc, Skyler & Alex. How do we convey the depth of our love and the profound gift of being your mothers? We have poured our hearts into these pages, striving to honor your memory in every word we share. We love you forever and always.

With heartfelt love and remembrance,

Melissa Bottorff-Arey

*"So many people are so much better off...
because they lived".*

Foreword

I first met Melissa in the summer of 2021 when I invited her to speak on my first interview series, *Healing After Suicide Loss*. I was very moved by her insights and connected with her on so many levels that she became a regular in my subsequent series.

Not only do we agree that time does *not* heal all wounds, but we also share a deep understanding of the brain science behind rewiring our neural pathways. Every time I hear Melissa speak on the topic of grief and suicide loss, I find myself nodding in agreement.

But that's not all. We both know what it's like to lose the mother-child bond, at least physically, to suicide – just from opposite perspectives. While Melissa lost her beloved son Alex when he was only 21 years old, I was only a couple of years older than him when I lost my dear Mum.

Although Melissa and I come from different experiences, we share a common understanding of the enduring impact of loss and the importance of honouring the memories of those we love.

We should never have to bury our children – it goes against the grain of nature. Even though I knew that my Mum was likely to leave this earth before me, I never expected to have her ripped away from me shortly after her 50th birthday and during my last year of university.

I may have technically been an adult, but I was still finding my feet in life. I miss my Mum deeply. I never really got to speak to her about pregnancy or having children because it wasn't something on my radar back then. Sadly, she never got to meet any of her grandchildren, but that doesn't mean that my children don't get to meet her.

They say we die twice – once when we draw our last breath and again when our name is mentioned for the last time. So, I talk to my children about my Mum and continue the same traditions, like baking Christmas cookies while listening to German Christmas music. It's by keeping these memories alive that we find comfort and strength.

I was in awe when Melissa first told me about her legacy project. What a beautiful way to keep a child's memory alive! It really is a testament to the love that never fades. It's her way of preserving the essence of a child's spirit and ensuring they are never forgotten.

In this book, you'll hear from Skyler's mom, Suzanne, Luc's mom, Sharon, and Alex's mom, my friend, Melissa.

First up is Skyler, who was incredibly kind, caring, and funny. He loved making memories with his siblings, whether dressing up, performing concerts, or being playful together. He had a passion for music and always showed up with warmth and humour. Skyler's big heart and vibrant spirit continue to inspire love and connection in everyone who knew him.

Then you'll meet Luc, who was full of energy and kindness, bringing joy to everyone around him. He was an athlete, a creative soul, and a loyal friend, excelling in everything from hockey and skiing to music and photography. Luc's warmth, adventurous spirit, and the special memories he created continue to inspire and comfort those who were lucky enough to know him. Both young men always gave 110% at whatever they did.

Last but not least, you'll meet Alex. If you have read the previous volumes of Because They Lived... (if you haven't, I highly recommend you do), you will have heard about the many stories shared by Melissa, as well as by others who love him so dearly. This book is no exception. You can look forward to getting to know Alex even better and in this volume get a few pearls of hard-earned wisdom from her grief journey as well.

And so, we are reminded that our loved ones are much more than how they died, and it is our duty and privilege to keep their memory alive.

Caro Brookings

Suicide Bereavement Coach and NeuroCoach

Table of Contents

———❤———

About This Book

———— ❤ ————

You are about to embark on a courageous journey. Opening this book to read these cherished memories and stories is a testament to your character and promises to be the grandest of adventures. I know this because I 'see' you. After we lose someone tragically, (re)visiting memories, even the good ones, can be painful and even brutal sometimes, right? But it's all part of the journey.

I can offer some solace, and insight as to how these moms even tackled this project to begin with. It starts with we can do hard things. Yes, we can. And yes, they are hard. As a matter of fact, I often say, *"hard things are hard,"* which seems like a redundant, somewhat 'duh' thing to say, but I have found that the reminder of 'this is going to be hard' - and preparing myself with all of the right tools - greatly helps my mindset, and ergo the outcome.

Think of it like this: if we set out to climb a mountain and put no thought into what lies ahead, and don't bring the right equipment, we can become overwhelmed and even quit at the first sign of 'hard' -- our mindset makes all the difference. We are less likely to give in to 'defeat' if we plan for and even 'embrace' the possibility of the worst.

Suicide wreaks havoc, no doubt, and still, by reading their stories, you may forget how they left this world. They are still 'here' between these covers— especially in our minds and hearts. Indeed, their vibrant spirits and souls are all around us, unceasingly. That, my friends, is how legacy works. Their life is what we remember and should remember; death is but a moment, legacy is enduring.

That brings me to discuss the enormous strength these moms mustered to take on and complete this book. And... let me acknowledge that I do not use a word like 'strength' lightly because being told how 'strong' we are is something most grievers hate. You may wonder why...well, we don't *feel* strong, and we don't *want* to be strong. We are surviving —only doing something that was thrust on us without choice—rising like phoenixes from instinct, not choice.

But, as I live in the glass house of a survivor, I can cast that stone: fortitude, backbone, and steadfastness. We can split hairs over any (inadequate) word, but it *is* strength, and they embrace it to face their most profound fear turned worst reality. I am immeasurably proud of them.

Just because we don't feel or want to be, doesn't mean we aren't (strong). Like the adrenaline rush that can help a human pick up a car in an emergency, our adrenaline (& cortisol) rush after loss also brings out a 'superhuman' buried-in-the-recesses strength that we may not otherwise feel we have, but it is there, nonetheless.

Sharon and Suzanne dug deep as moms do and did *all* of the hard work this project calls for-- and they benefited, but now, so will you. So will the many people who go on to be impacted by the life stories of these young men. Sharon and Suzanne have helped prove why I believe mothers' rule the world.' I am not alone:

> "*Mothers and their children are in a category all their own. There's no bond so strong in the entire world.*" - unknown.

"Men are what their mothers made them."-Ralph Waldo Emerson

"When love is gone, there's always justice. And when justice is gone, there's always force. And when force is gone, there's always Mom. Hi, Mom!"—Laurie Anderson

"The unsung heroes of the civil rights movement were always the wives and the mothers." A. Young

As you get to know (or become re-familiar with) Skyer, Luc, and Alex, you will be entertained, you may shed tears, and will definitely be inspired. There are so many takeaways in this book—and they are remembered, and their names are spoken—legacy for the win!

This initiative blends elements of narrative therapy with writing to assist grieving moms as they navigate their healing journey while penning a magic-filled chapter dedicated to their child. Each mother receives total support throughout the process, fostering emotional recovery and an authentic representation of their shared experiences. This book is a source of inspiration, showcasing the profound healing that can come from storytelling and connection.

Whatever your reason for reading this book, know that you are not alone. If *you* struggle and are searching for a reason to stay, let *this* be it. *Here's your sign from the Universe.* Stay. You are loved and needed by so many. I hope these stories, these lives, help those of you who need to realize the permanence of suicide and hear how much everyone would miss you every day, forever. Life can always get better.

Now, as always, here I am--at the place in the book where I always end up--the place of asking you to hug the grieving mom(s) in your life. Hug them a little longer, even tighter, every next chance you get. Carrying the pain of child loss is the hardest, and often the loneliest, thing we will ever do in our lives. Unlike most grief, this never ends. We have no logical place to 'put' this, so we learn to carry it. Hugs are a simple yet powerful way to show support and provide comfort (--that *and continuing to talk about their child*).

Now, take a moment to get in the mindset and collect the 'tools' you need and settle into a comfy spot, whether snuggled up on a cozy sofa, sitting beneath a towering tree, or reclined on a blanket by the sea. These fantastic stories are best experienced with an open mind and a loving heart.

As you read, you hold the past and present in your hands, and by absorbing and sharing these stories with others, you play a role in shaping the future. May you find solace, understanding, and even hope within these pages. Thank you for being a part of this journey with us.

It's going to be an adventure, and you'll be so glad you embarked on it with us!

Skyler Augustus Little
September 1, 2000 - March 27, 2024

Skyler

Snow White's Prince

Losing a child is, by far, the worst thing that can ever occur to a parent or a family. Additionally, suicide loss adds an even deeper complication, as survivors often experience questioning, blame, and a basic lack of understanding of themselves, and our society. As I work (from my trauma space) to remember how he lived and not just focus on how he died, I have both joy and sadness peek in. It is now and always will be a double-edged sword to remember Skyler. As long as I am breathing, I will say his name and speak his truth to keep his memory alive and with us.

After we lose someone close to us, it is expected that many memories of that person will flood back into our minds, including stories that we have not thought of in years. Suicide loss is no different, but at the same time, survivors often analyze every memory, trying to determine what was missed. Did we miss a hint or an opportunity to enjoy a moment with our loved one? One of my last interactions with Skyler was a phone call a few weeks before his death.

He shared with me his joy because he felt like he was on a good path – he was happy in his relationship, had a new job, and had recently adopted a new four-legged family member. I was elated to hear the excitement in his voice. Now, I wonder if he was protecting me by not sharing his struggles with me.

It amazes me that I can recall some things clearly, but I cannot hardly call to mind the day that life was altered forever –the day that I was told that Skyler was no longer on this earth. I now know that this was my brain's way of protecting me, in a way 'insulating' me from the awful details of that day, but it's still unsettling to have my mind feel 'hijacked.' Yet, I have no trouble remembering how excited we were when we learned we were expecting Skyler.

We had all of the 'typical' questions. How would he get along with his older sister? What would his personality be like? Who would he look like? What would his passions be? A new life typically brings joy, hope, and happiness to the child's parents. In our case, bringing Skyler into the world was a blessing, and my husband and I met it with all of the optimism and love in the world.

He was our second born child, and he was loved and wanted before we even knew we were pregnant. I recall anticipating him to arrive and how he would be another incredible piece of our growing family.

What joy and hope we had for him before and at his birth! Like in that famous children's story, we loved him "...*to the moon and back*." I recall that early on, Skyler loved sleeping while he was held skin-to-skin. He appeared more relaxed and content when his dad or I held him. Skyler would often be startled awake whenever we attempted to transition him to his crib or bassinet, and he seemed to "need" that reassurance from close contact with mom or dad. Of course, we were delighted to hold and nurture him however he preferred.

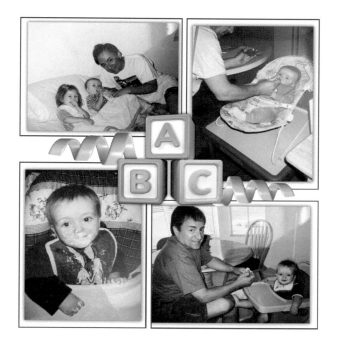

Sandwiched between an older sister and several younger brothers, he watched his older sister and enjoyed their interactions. Even when Skyler was an infant, anything she did fascinated him. Luckily, she was equally excited to engage with him and often 'read' or sang to him.

The early days of us as a family of four were filled with so much joy as we all fell into our new routines of being together. As he grew, he was content to play what she wanted and accepted her direction in games and pretend play. I can very clearly remember him following her around and engaging in any activity she was interested in, including playing with dolls, dress-up, or any other activity she dreamed up. The two of them often put on 'concerts' for us, singing their favorite songs from the cartoons they enjoyed

When Skyler and his younger brothers were preschool age, they often played dress-up and pretend games under the watchful tutelage of their older sister. At times, this included dressing up in princess costumes at the direction of said sister. Older sisters can be one part fun and one part ornery that way. Seeing him dressed up as Snow White (his favorite princess at the time), Cinderella, or Ariel was priceless. He would don the whole 'shebang' – dress, wig, and high-heels and follow his sister around the house. Smiling ear-to-ear, Skyler had tea parties and played house, all under the watchful eye of his older sister. He idolized her at that age and was game to participate in any activity she concocted. I adore these happy memories of them all being so close and enjoying each other's company. As one of his brothers recently told me:

"I always looked up to Skyler when we were young and learned from him since he was the first of us boys to get to do things like get a job and drive. I remember when all of us younger guys had our first jobs, and Skyler would often drive us to work on his way to work. He always worked hard and wanted to do the right thing."

Fast forward several years, and the 'student' became the 'teacher.' His sister had taught him well, and where his younger brothers were concerned, Skyler soon became the leader of the pack. It was his turn to guide, so the princess costumes were retired, and instead, he led the boys in pretend play like 'cops and robbers,' sports, or other rough and tumble activities. One of the favorite activities that my boys enjoyed was 'sliding' down the stairs of our two-story home. Looking back, it is impressive that they did not all break a bone as they tried to best one another in sliding faster or more 'creatively' than each other.

Even when he was young, Skyler was patient with his younger brothers, including one of his brothers, who had some delays in communication skills. He would sometimes 'talk' for his brother to help him communicate better, especially with unfamiliar listeners. It was so touching as a mama to watch, and I think being on the (high functioning) end of the autism spectrum himself, Skyler had an innate compassion for his brother's struggles. He also enjoyed taking on a leadership role with all of his brothers- sometimes for good and other times into more 'misguided' activities- as they looked up to him and eagerly followed his lead.

Usually, their play was energetic and stayed 'in bounds.' Yet, sometimes, it led to creative, though not always well-thought-out activities – such as 'redecorating' their bedrooms or dressing up the (*very* tolerant) pets. Even though he was not much older than his four younger brothers, they all were enthralled with him at that age and loved following in his footsteps in every activity he undertook. When he wanted to play basketball, they followed suit, and when he started school, the younger boys all cried when he left in the mornings and asked for him during the day until he returned in the afternoon.

As Skyler and (some) of his brothers moved into high school, a few became heavily involved in theater. Even though he was not interested in performing, Skyler wanted to support his brothers in their love for theater. Not to be outdone, he helped alongside his dad, a volunteer for the musical theater program, by assisting with ticket sales and serving as an usher to seat those who came to see the shows.

He was so proud to see his brothers perform and loved that he was able to assist in some way. Skyler would dress in his finest to help patrons find their seats and was delighted to support his brothers.

Skyler's willingness to help was evident in so many ways. Skyler loved to help us around the house, even as a young child. If only all kids were like this! As a little boy, he 'worked' with me and his dad when we cleaned the house. Many kids enjoy pretending to do what mom and dad do around the house, but Skyler took his role seriously. As soon as he was old enough, we worked side-by-side, and he even took on chores, appearing to enjoy the responsibility. As his parents, we were always grateful for his help and enjoyed that special time with him. As he grew older, it turned out that cleaning served a different purpose.

As a teen, he struggled with anxiety and seemed to have a sense of calm when he was engaged in household tasks. I can clearly recall him spontaneously cleaning around the home without being asked. When I talked to him about this over the years, he said, "*Mom, I feel like I am taking control over things when I clean, which helps me feel less anxious.*" While I always appreciated his willingness to help, and I was proud that he had found a coping skill, it also broke my mama-heart to know he was driven to do this as a way to harness the deep feelings and anxiety that troubled him - things that would go on to create bigger troubles as the years progressed.

Skyler

The pattern continued– and as soon as he was old enough, he found an (real) job to help occupy that part of him that needed to be busy (aka 'distracted'). Proud of his work, he was always considered a contributing team member, no matter his role. Skyler typically went above and beyond in assigned tasks. It seemed he was seeking external feedback to help him feel whole, as he also struggled with self-esteem. He often excelled in these jobs as he had a tremendous work ethic and beamed when others recognized his efforts.

To this point, the principal at his former high school shared this sentiment with me, stating, "Skyler was always ready with a smile and a helping hand."

He initially worked in restaurants and hotels and later worked for the county government. When describing my son, 'all-in' or '110%' - both fit, and others readily agreed.

From the time he was a baby, my son was a deep thinker who often preferred to be alone. At a very young age, he frequently appeared to be 'lost in his thoughts.' Skyler had only a few close friends but many acquaintances throughout childhood and into adulthood. He often told me that being around others he did not know well was particularly stressful. He ultimately didn't know what to say and just wanted to say the 'right thing.'

We would role-play with him when he was young and into adolescence to help prepare him for anxious social situations. This calmed him as it helped him feel prepared for specific interactions. Of course, we could never prepare him for everything that could happen, which continued to be a source of distress as the years progressed. Even though social situations could be a challenge, Skyler did not shy away from putting himself out there with regard to taking jobs. Intent on overcoming his social anxiety, he would always strive to continue to grow in this area.

At one point, he worked as a bellman at a resort in our community. By this time, he was a young adult, and his stress with social situations followed him into this role. To help him with his social anxiety, we would give him 'talking points' to share with resort guests while he escorted them to their rooms. This position helped him grow significantly in his confidence and willingness to engage socially with others. He would love to come home and share stories about customers he had assisted.

Skyler also got immediate reinforcement for his hard work through generous tips from the resort guests. He loved telling his brothers about how much he earned in tips after each shift, and they were amazed at the 'good luck' their brother had with getting just the right guest that he 'clicked with' as he ushered them to their room.

My boy had a unique perspective on life in general, and at times, he struggled to see things from another's point of view. He would often come home from school asking us to help him 'replay' moments from his day to assist him in understanding them better. Even at home, he sometimes struggled to know if someone was teasing him and needed explanations for phrases and comments that were not literal.

I am glad he was so comfortable coming to us to help him navigate communication challenges, which continued into adulthood. However, like many young adults, there were struggles that he kept to himself, maybe to protect us as parents.

With communication as such a great stressor for Skyler, the result was that it caused him significant anxiety. I can still 'see' the often perplexed expression on his face as he was trying to figure out a situation. A new problem cropped up when, as a teen and young adult, Skyler learned to mask his true feelings quite well and generally had a smile on his face. Initially, I saw his smile as mischievous and wondered what he was up to. It was when he got older that I realized he was trying to 'match' others' expressions and that his smile could simply be a cover for his anxiety - in my memory, it was an uncomfortable smile. Years later, it breaks my heart to think of him trying to decipher others' true intentions while hiding behind that charming, somewhat unsure grin.

Despite it all, Skyler also had great humor and loved joking with his siblings. Of course, like most young boys, sometimes his sense of humor was inappropriate in nature or timing. When he was younger, he and his brothers loved 'bathroom humor,' especially if it was offensive or embarrassing to their older sister. At times, Skyler and his brothers appeared to try to say things that they knew would embarrass their older sister. Thankfully, as he matured, so did his sense of humor - enjoying typical adolescent and young adult humor but also developing a more beyond-his-years, dry humor. His quick wit could always make me laugh - even when it was somewhat inappropriate.

When our two youngest children joined our family by adoption, with Skyler and his brothers all in high school, we, as parents, reminded the older kids how impressionable 'little ears' can be. Skyler outdid himself in finding creative ways to be funny while not (obviously) using any inappropriate language around his two youngest siblings, and he would quickly correct his brothers if they said anything inappropriate within earshot of his youngest siblings. There were so many instances of his dad and I trying not to laugh at something Skyler did. As it turned out, he knew this and seemed to really enjoy it when I could not hold back my laughter, even at the inappropriate comments. I can still see him with a twinkle in his eye, grinning back at me when he knew he had made me crack my (typically) more stoic exterior.

In those famed dress-up sessions with his older sister, Skyler became quite practiced at 'transforming' into his favorite Disney princesses. When he was three, our family went on a Disney Cruise, and Skyler joined the other preschoolers in the kid's activity center, where part of that experience was meeting Disney characters. He was thrilled! One evening, when we picked Skyler up from the children's

center, he had a lipstick 'kiss' on his cheek. As soon as he saw us, he was beaming with excitement and ready to share his evening adventures. Seeing the 'kiss' on his cheek, we waited to let him share, and he could not have been prouder to tell the whole story.

It seems that evening, Snow White visited the children in the kids' activity center, and our son, being very smitten with this princess in particular, apparently did not leave her side.

He was so serious about this event that he did not want us to 'wash off' the kiss, proceeding to tell anyone who would listen all about it for the entire remainder of the voyage. The pure joy of that experience continues to be one of my favorite memories of Skyler as a young child. This event caused him to be even more enthralled with the said princess for years after this, and it became a favorite family story even as he grew older. When he was a preteen and teen, we often asked him when he would meet 'his' Snow White. I adored that he was always a good sport and did not become frustrated with us anytime that we retold this story.

I always knew he was a bright and capable learner. Even before he started school, we knew we had a little smarty on our hands. As a preschooler, he excelled in picking up vocabulary and problem-solving and could get into (and out of) everything. If we tried to keep him out of certain areas, he would devise a way to get around every 'keep-Skyler-out' contraption we came up with. And, true to form, he would lead the way, and his brothers would fall into line, right on his heels. It would be impossible to recount how often he and his brothers got into mischief as it was more the rule and less the exception at that point.

A particular memory is when Skyler and his brothers 'found' one of Santa's hiding places just a few short days before Christmas. Despite our best efforts, it was challenging to keep the gifts from Santa hidden from our big brood. Once the 'cat was out of the bag,' we concocted a story about how Santa had to make an early delivery because his sleigh could not hold all the gifts that year. Thankfully, this satisfied them in the short term and did not ruin the magic of Christmas - at least not prematurely.

As I have alluded, he was academically at or near the top of his class. Not only did he catch on quickly, but he applied himself fully, loving that recognition so much. Even though we, as parents, only encouraged him to do whatever *his* best was, Skyler seemed to always naturally set his sights on being *the* best. In many cases, it paid off, and Skyler even earned the honor of being the valedictorian of his high school class.

Now, with this honor, he would be expected to give a speech at graduation, and he was instantly ready to reconsider whether the honor was truly worth it. Writing the speech that he wanted to deliver to encourage his fellow graduates to strive for success came easy enough; however, *delivering* the speech was a different story. It took pep talks from us, teachers, and friends, but he pulled it off, proud to have simply gotten through it as he would later convey. It seemed that he was beginning to learn to be comfortable in his own skin as he aged—or so it seemed.

During his junior and senior years of high school, Skyler also took dual enrollment courses, initially making him quite anxious, and he needed much encouragement. Of course, with his strong work ethic and keen intellect, success followed, leading to more confidence and success in future classes. As it would turn out, these dual enrollment courses served another purpose for my son – helping him become more self-aware and even more vital in self-advocacy.

The power and privilege of being allowed to witness (and now recall and share) these things as a parent still humbles me.

Once, Skyler took a course in American Sign Language as part of this dual enrollment coursework. He was eager to learn this skill and took great pride in developing proficiency in basic sign language.

The state school for the deaf and blind was located in our community, and he had grown accustomed to seeing sign language used regularly in our town. Skyler was excited and saw this as his opportunity to learn to communicate with members of the community who are deaf.

family

forever

love

Playing in the orchestra was a commitment many of the kids in our family made over the years. Skyler was no exception. He and his older sister had more interest and, thus, more commitment to the orchestra than their younger siblings. They continued to be involved in community orchestra well into high school. Skyler played upright bass, and his sister played viola.

While both in high school, they took private lessons and joined the community orchestra, which was comprised primarily of adults. Skyler was always diligent in caring for his instrument and practicing regularly, showing maturity beyond his years –thriving in this environment – to the point that he seemed more comfortable with adults than his peers. He loved performing in concerts and dressing up for the performances. It was beautiful to see him full of joy and 'in the zone' when he was playing his bass.

As a young child, Skyler was like most boys his age, less concerned with his appearance, and more with comfort, dressing mostly in active wear and t-shirts. However, once he hit middle school, that casual perspective on attire changed and suddenly he wanted to dress 'nicer'. His dad worked a job requiring him to dress in a shirt and tie daily. Skyler looked up to his dad and wanted to dress nicely for specific occasions like holidays and special events. He was so proud of himself when he dressed formally for orchestra concerts and when he learned to tie his necktie! He looked like such a little 'man' when he was all dressed up. He loved that he could dress like Dad, distinguishing himself even more as a leader among his siblings.

In physical appearance, he resembled his paternal grandfather. He was never able to meet him, but Skyler was so proud that he looked like him and enjoyed looking at photos of Grandpa and pointing out their similarities. Skyler's broad shoulders, strength, height, and facial features reflected Grandpa's attributes. He was always interested in hearing stories about extended family members and was our number one 'researcher' in family genealogy projects. I have found some comfort in moments knowing that my husband and his parents were there to greet Skyler when he left this earth.

To those who did not know him well, Skyler presented as reserved, which might come across as aloof or uninterested. If you knew him, it was to see that he was riveted and passionate about many things. You would only know this side of him, though, if he trusted you - was comfortable with you – not just anyone got a glimpse of this side. He had such an advanced vocabulary and mature thoughts even as an adolescent, and if you were part of the 'inner circle' of trust, he openly shared ideas with you.

It was a joy to have conversations with Skyler and to hear his complex and exciting perspective on various topics. I loved having those in-depth discussions with him and was amazed at seeing him grow from an infant babbler to a bigger person, having advanced conversations using big words. I found such pleasure hearing his perspective on quite the variety of subjects and enjoyed seeing another side of things by delving in with him. Now, I miss these opportunities to engage and hear his varying views.

One of these passions began as a way of showing he cared and developed into a way to help others. Skyler's love of cooking and baking was a fun way for his zealous side to manifest. Skyler had always loved to be a kitchen helper, but as a preteen and teen, he became more independent and creative. Like his comfort with cleaning, Skyler also found solace in the satisfaction of task completion and the often solitary nature of cooking and baking. He regularly treated the family to any number of desserts, finding himself calmer and more relaxed.

Chef Skyler

Skyler was most famous for his baking; he particularly loved baking pies. He was so proud of his work in the kitchen, and we certainly appreciated his efforts! I remember that even extended family members would rave about Skyler's pies at family gatherings. During his high school years, he even participated in the culinary arts program at his school, where he could learn hands-on skills and earn certifications that could only help as he moved into the workforce.

The culinary students could participate in a community project to feed the local homeless population every season. Oh, how Skyler's spirit shined through! He and his classmates planned the meal, prepared the dishes, and served it to some of the local homeless population at our community center. He participated in this event each time that he had the opportunity. Skyler spoke about how he saw the individuals he was serving when many people in our culture look through or around those who are homeless. He had deep compassion and respect for those he served, and I am so proud of Skyler and his love for and willingness to serve others. Of course, as parents, we often learn from our children. I never found the homeless population to be aversive, but Skyler helped me learn to see each person through his lens and to see his respect for the homeless population in our community.

Besides cooking, the family pets also held a piece of my son's heart and enthusiasm. Enthralled by animals as far back as I can remember, Skyler would watch our family pets, mesmerized by them even as an infant. When he was young, he was always so gentle with the animals. As he grew, Skyler wanted to help with their overall care and would regularly feed them. As he became more and more independent in caring for our pets, he frequently told us what our pets were 'thinking.' Hearing his take on what they were 'saying' to him was priceless. Skyler took on a large part of pet care in our family as he got older. His devotion to our 'furry kids' was unmatched, so I wasn't surprised when he carried this love into adulthood. Even as a young man living independently with his own pets to care for, he would still frequently come by to help with the fur babies in our home.

In thinking of this impassioned side of my son, along with music, learning, and cooking, I also think of Legos and trip planning - he was a natural builder and explorer. However, most of all, we were a Disney family long before we had children. Disney has always had a special place in our hearts as a couple, and we raised our children to love Disney as well. Skyler was no exception to the family 'rule' and loved so many of the characters from a young age.

He had that love for Snow White, and from there, as Skyler grew up, he showed his 'Disney love' by watching movies and collecting pins. In fact, he acquired an extensive pin collection and prided himself on how many he had.

When he was older, Skyler's favorite character became Goofy, and he especially loved eating at Chef Mickey's Restaurant at Disney World, which fit with his growing love for

cooking. As it seemed, Goofy was one of Mickey's Sous Chefs, which made him love him all the more!

For the Love of Disney

When you wish upon a star... ...your dreams come true

My husband absolutely loved the holidays, especially Christmas. He always went above and beyond to make the day extra special. This passion for the holidays did not skip a generation because our kids love Christmas, too. However, like his dad, Skyler loved Christmas and making those he loved happy during the holidays. When our children were young, my husband bought a Santa suit and donned it yearly to 'get caught sneaking into the house.' The children were delighted, and this brought them so much joy! Not to be outdone, when his youngest two siblings were little, Skyler volunteered to be Santa for them. The joy on his face as he shared his idea with us was immense. Seeing his excitement, his dad graciously agreed to pass on that honor to Skyler. As Christmas Eve was approaching, Skyler made his plan for exactly how he would surprise his siblings. He did not miss a beat and made Santa's visit to our house magical for our two youngest children.

A very favorite thing about my incredible son was his kind heart, especially when he frequently showed how much he cared for others who were struggling in some way he could relate to. Whether the struggle is with development, such as autism spectrum disorder or other delays, or with mental health, Skyler seemed to have a built-in love, or empathy, for others who had a struggle in life. We witnessed this firsthand with Skyler and his siblings. He was very tolerant and warm towards his youngest brother, who is on the autism spectrum. While his brother is only moderately impacted by this condition, there is nothing moderate about Skyler's compassion.

From the start, Skyler devoted his time and efforts to his youngest brother to help him adjust to our family and to bond with him. Even though there was an age difference, Skyler got down on his brother's level and made a point to get to know his brother's areas of interest. He was also very generous and regularly got surprises for his youngest siblings. Skyler would get the kids' favorite candy or a book with their favorite character. He even got them a bounce house during the early stages of the pandemic to give the kids something to do to keep them active during those months of lockdown.

It, in fact, seemed that Skyler, even more so than some of his siblings, immediately made a connection with his youngest brother when he joined our family through adoption – once again demonstrating a depth of understanding that seemed to be more *with* his brother and not as much *for* him. Even when his brother struggled to communicate, Skyler appeared to just 'know' how to be of the most help. This loving, all-understanding quality is one of Skyler's super-powers that will continue as part of his legacy – it is woven into the fabric of our family's tapestry. To be his mama has been such an incredible gift.

"You just call out my name..."

"He ain't heavy...he's my brother"

and you know wherever I am.
I'll come running..."

I love all of these amazing memories, and it is critical not to focus on the single moment of how he died but more on these memories from the years that he lived. This is my purpose in writing. He lived such a vibrant, rich life, and I want to honor that by remembering and sharing these stories and memories of who he was in life and who he still is in spirit.

I have discovered that it's easy for grievers to only think about their loss and, in the case of suicide, especially how our loved one died. The depth of trauma and grief after a loss such as this is immense. Having suffered two significant losses in only eight months, I find myself vacillating among many emotions, and often more than one feeling shows up. As I ride the waves of grief and the accompanying emotions, I am making a choice to continue to strive to be on the celebrating side of the life that Skyler lived.

As I sit here, I realize the weight of my responsibility as the 'keeper of our memories.' It now falls upon me to share with my surviving children and the world the remarkable individuals that Skyler *and* Skip, his father, were and still are in spirit. I do see our family like a tapestry woven with beautiful, forever-intertwined threads. As the family story continues, the patterns become more robust and vibrant. But life, like any tapestry, can also show signs of wear and tear; it's the natural course of life. Lives, like stories, don't always end as we hope, but it is my self-appointed 'job' to ensure that I preserve and protect the uniqueness of each thread of this heart-woven masterpiece that represents my son and my husband - one lost to suicide but both now gone from my grasp.

Skyler was an intensely loving individual who poured 110% of his heart into everything he did. His life, though brief, was steeped in the passion he shared for the people he loved and his diverse interests – friends, family, pets, Legos, Disney, and helping others, all of which are just a few of the many things he cherished. Skyler's presence in our family is permanently sewn in -- things such as his quick wit, dedicated efforts, and kind nature -- but like all of us, he was not without his struggles.

My son's challenges with chronic anxiety and awkward social skills, at times, left him at a loss for how to engage – sometimes even with us. He worked so hard to overcome his difficulties, and at the same time, Skyler often questioned where he stood with others. His doubts impacted his decision-making skills, and Skyler's deep thinking sometimes took him to troubling, and even dark places. Skyler's intellect, deep, intense feelings, and strong sense of fairness (or lack thereof) steered his perspective and challenged us as parents and a family. In the end, I know this was his undoing.

It was sometimes challenging. In fact, there were downright hard years *and* also so many, many good ones. The 'ands' are so relevant in this life after loss. I am so delighted to have been his mama *and* it was sometimes a real challenge. I am slowly learning to honor *and* balance it all.

Most importantly, I do know Skyler was loved deeply, from the deepest place in a mama's heart, and I know he knew this. These two things make me feel secure, softly comforted, and eternally grateful. I love you, my boy—*to the moon and back*!

Luc Josef Barron

September 20, 2005 - September 24, 2022

Luc

The Making of a Goalie

Dearest Luc,

It breaks my heart to find myself writing your legacy; your father and I are still in disbelief. You should be writing ours. You also should be in your first year of college, and we should be missing you for that reason. You might have gone to Michigan State like your dad did, or maybe Michigan like your big sister? You had so many choices to make. But that was not to be our family path; instead, you were abruptly taken from us two years ago, on September 24, 2022. And here we are, without you.

To say that the past two years have been extremely challenging is the greatest of understatements. I've grasped many things to help me understand and move forward without you physically here, most of which have been colossal failures.

At this point, part of me wants to remain in disbelief, even denial. It feels best to think that you are not physically present with me but rather that you are out there, still on earth, somewhere. Yet you are not, and I know this strategy will only serve me in the short run. So, I choose to step forward, bringing you with me. I write about your life (your legacy) to keep you close but also to help in my healing as I learn to successfully live alongside this grief.

As part of this writing journey, I also talked with others and asked them to write about you, too. You are so loved, and many of them obliged. Luc, the following chapter contains some of these memories and stories expressed through me, your mother, your father's help, and so many of the people you touched in your all-too-short time with us. These contributions help us all remember your life more fully, and I am eternally grateful.

I look back to that day—just four days after you turned 17 years old, on what seemed like a typical September Saturday morning—and I still think, "How?" You took off on a bike, leaving your phone behind; we would never see you again after that bike ride. The 'what could we have done 'or 'how we could have helped' are gone with you. You should be here, and yet, you are not.

Now, in this new, unwelcome, unbelievable version of life, I often feel like I am living outside of my own body, even though I do actually know that it is my body—my reality—it is a reality for all of us who love you. So, I choose to lean into healing by leaning into your life; now, we turn to remembering and keeping you with us. Now, we tell your story.

Forever Love For You, Mom

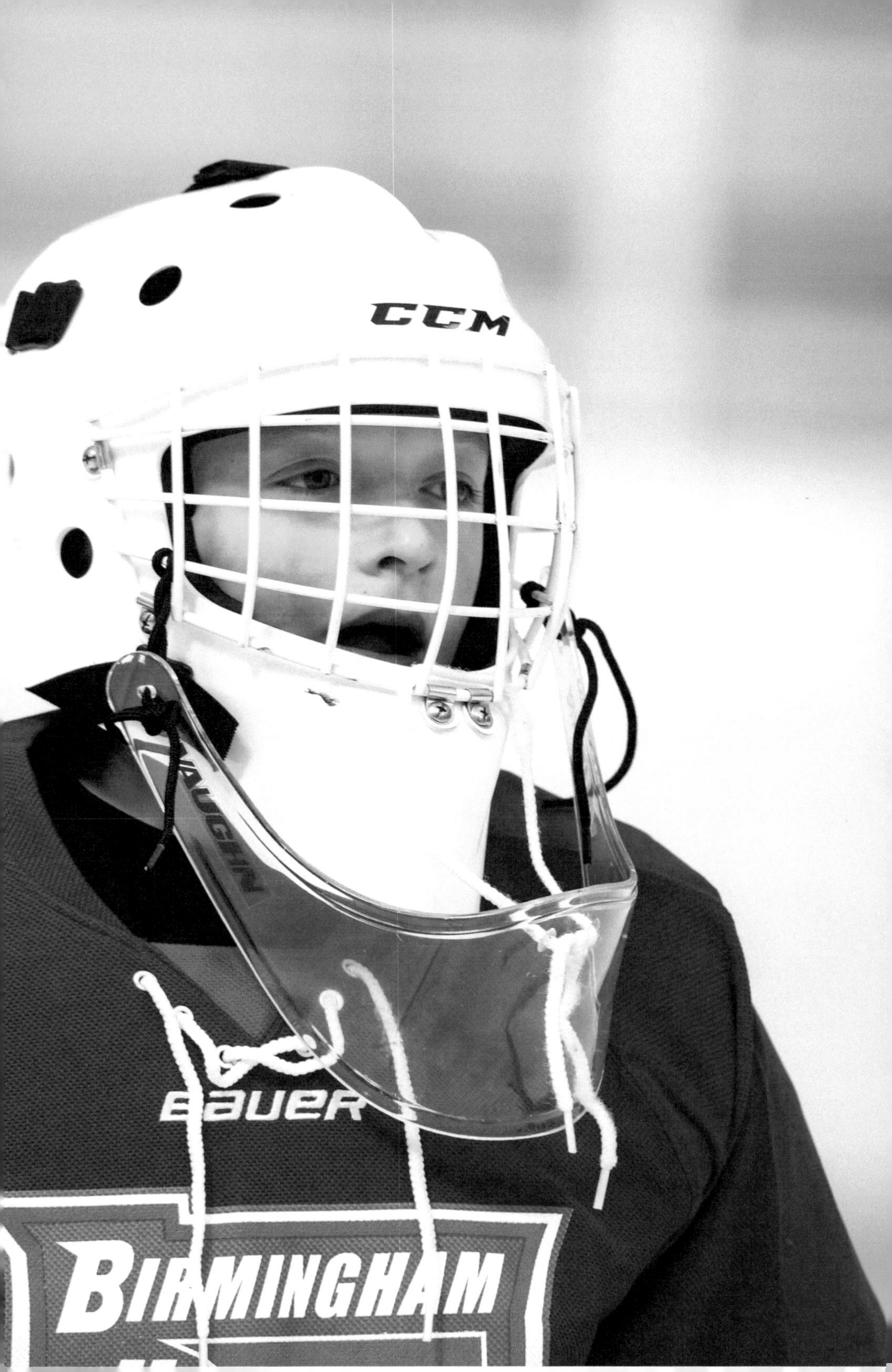
CCM
VAUGHN
BAUER
BIRMINGHAM

After becoming a doctor, all I wanted to be was a mom and give my husband a son, and on a routine prenatal ultrasound, we saw the 'quarterback view' of his gender... unmistakably male. I burst into joyful tears, and Luc was bouncing on the ultrasound with my happy sobs. As his mom, I vowed to love and protect him for my entire life and the bulk of his. Alas, that was not to be, and I was only given 17 years and 4 days to love, see, touch, and just know my beautiful son.

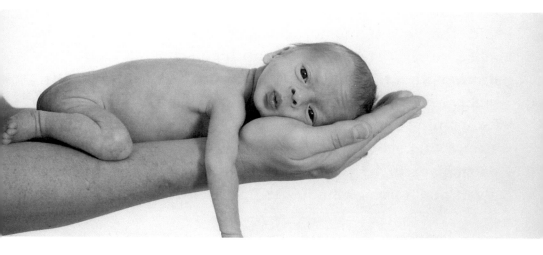

In 2005, Luc Josef Barron was born five weeks prematurely on a September Tuesday night via Cesarean section. The obstetrician was monitoring the womb for placenta previa, and my 35-week ultrasound showed an underweight baby. He needed to be delivered soon and rescued by skilled doctors and nurses. Moved by the drama and outcome, my husband and I named our son Luc in honor of the medical staff that was responsible for his survival. 'Luke' is an Apostle and the Saint of Doctors in the Catholic church. Therefore, we named him 'Luc' - and spelled his name in the three-letter form honoring the French heritage of his surname, Barron.

While trying to conceive, dad thought adding a male black lab puppy to our family was a good idea and so came Bruno. He felt that Bruno would be a pal to our young female black lab, Raven and that he might help me not be disappointed if the third IVF attempt failed. Well, I became pregnant shortly after we got Bruno, and I spent the rest of my pregnancy raising this new puppy. Which was OK with me because Bruno loved taking naps like I did and curled beside me on the couch with Luc in my tummy.

It seems logical to start with Luc as a baby, but, truth be told, the newest memories linger in the foreground a bit more, so we'll start there - with high school. Luc attended Brother Rice High School (BRHS,) his dad's alma mater; a highly regarded Catholic college prep school well known for its winning sports teams. It was a 'no-brainer' for him to attend this school, and Luc believed it was a privilege to participate in it; parents paid tuition, scholarships were given, and it was a school with Christian values.

A Mother's Love is Eternal

Paraphrasing Luc from his 9th-grade school journal, he said his high school goals are '*to get good grades, get into a good college, have a starting position on the BRHS hockey team, and learn more about the church, and get closer to God.*' He had a solid moral compass and believed that respect and kindness were how you proudly represent yourself and your school. However, if he witnessed bullying or students disrespecting teachers, he would be very disappointed, often telling me and his dad the story later. Also disturbing to him was the behavior of a few particular stereotypical bully-ish 'jocks' pushing their way into groups forming for a project. He often formed a group with the remaining students. I am proud that Luc was athletic but, indeed, not a typical 'jock.'

Athleticism is often the first thing others will remember about Luc. It is still funny to me that hockey has become his primary sport. His dad never played it, and I certainly didn't know a thing about it. It was a 'Michigan thing.' I remember bringing Luc to a rink to learn to skate at three years old. It was a wonder that any kids could even stand up; it was like a bunch of baby seals in clothes, sliding around the ice on their backs and stomachs. I took note: all the other boys were so intent on scoring, but my Luc was the only one who worked to defend and stay behind while the others crashed the net. From the beginning, I watched as a goalie was born, sparking a nostalgic connection to his early interest in hockey!

I went to most of Luc's hockey games, sometimes in my doctor's scrubs out of time-saving necessity to get there as soon as possible, so I didn't miss the 'hockey puck drop' (which I quickly learned was 'a thing'). I don't think he minded because as soon as he saw me, we shared a Luc-mom-head nod that was our unique gesture. No matter what arena he was playing at, I would stand near and watch him play as close to the goalie net as possible. It's always exciting, albeit finger-nail-biting, as a mom to watch her son block a goal or see a puck slam into the net for the other team's goal. Who knew...it seems that destiny had a hand and that being a 'hockey mom' was always a part of my plan.

As a hockey parent, we would learn that, generally, it's not good when your child chooses to be a goalie. The equipment is expensive and tedious to care for; your kid plays the whole game or not at all, and often, the win or loss rests on just one or two saves or misses by the goalie. It is nerve-racking. But in retrospect, Luc was made to do it. Dad was typically running the scoreboard and sound system, and mom would often join him to be able to experience games from both the players' and parents' perspectives.

In fact, at times, I would join him so I could be close to the action. Luc was just different from the other kids on the team, somehow more focused, always giving it his all. We discussed how Luc would play a 'different' game than the other players. If the team was getting their butts kicked, Luc was enjoying it as the action was all around him; he was getting 'peppered' (with pucks) and, strangely, having a great time of it.

He often played a separate contest in his head in tight games– something not lost on his coaches over the years, elaborating on his performance. When most nervous, he would overcome to play well, make saves, put up shutouts, and win hockey games. He always gave 110% to support his team and did not appear upset with a loss as long as he played well. In between periods when goalies changed ends, he would nod and have that sparkle in his eye as he locked in when the puck dropped. He was calm during games and never let a bad game or goal bother him. With his quiet confidence, he instilled trust in his teammates, making them believe they could win any game with Luc at the goal.

Over the years, Luc played with many of the same boys on each hockey team, whether from Birmingham house teams or travel hockey. Ultimately, playing at BRHS as a 9th-10th grade goalie on the junior varsity team and filled in on the varsity team when they didn't have a goalie. Unfortunately, it didn't appear that Luc would play up to Varsity in the 11th grade at BRHS because two goalies who had been playing on outside AAA travel teams would now play for BRHS, and a third would not be needed. They had priority.

Being unable to play broke Luc's heart, and for some of the other reasons I previously mentioned, Luc switched schools at the beginning of 11th grade. Because of the transfer, Michigan High School hockey regulations required him to sit out a season before he could play again for the Birmingham Unified Kings in 2023. He could attend all practices in 2022, but Luc left this earth before this could happen.

Now, let's visit those younger athletic years, before hockey, where skiing was something else that my Luc mastered. Starting at four years of age, he learned in Michigan and Park City, Utah, as his sisters had. His sisters learned to snowboard, but Luc was only interested in snow skiing, just

like his dad. He was adorable when he was three feet tall, wearing his ski helmet, looking like he might just topple over. The five of us 'rode' the mountain together, and as Luc grew into a tween, he got very fast and began to go off with friends or by himself.

Luc once shared a story - he was skiing in Park City, Utah - a friend and he decided to go to Jupiter Peak at 11,000 feet. Coming down, they got lost in a valley and could

only hike while carrying their skies to get out. They spent five hours hiking and skiing to return to the mountain base. His last ski trip was in February 2022, when he and his dad visited Vail, Colorado. Oh, how I wish that I would have gone with them. This is the thing, once someone we love is gone, all chances for more memories are lost with them.

Luc

Luc Barror

Lacrosse was another sport he played from age 9 to 13. Like in hockey, he was a natural defender; he seemed more interested in protecting the goal than scoring the goals. However, unlike hockey, Luc had no interest in being a goalie; instead, he played a defensive midfielder position. It's not that he didn't score goals; he did, but he was known for his tenacious defense and his exceptional ability to move the ball down the field with either his stick or his legs.

He had strong arms to catch and throw the ball with the lacrosse stick, blocking the opponent's sticks until he could pass. He could run like a deer, and once, he wore my Fitbit during practice. How does 10,000 steps in one hour sound?

Luc was also an avid swimmer; starting at four, he grew up with a backyard pool. He wore goggles and swam underwater like a fish. He loved to dive to get the pool toy that sank to the bottom. He and his friends would put floats under the diving board and laugh as they jumped onto the floats and watched them fly everywhere. Cannonballs off the diving board by dad always delighted the kids with a big splash. Dad also threw balls to Luc, whereas Luc jumped high off the diving board into the air and one-handedly caught the ball midair before entering the water—Luc with laser eyes, which, as it turned out, were also quite suitable for being a hockey goalie and online gaming.

Antics at the Lake

Summer Fun

Each summer, we would spend time with family and friends at Torch Lake, Michigan, at his friend Ryan's place. He typically brought another friend of his along. Ethan was often a popular guest. The boys enjoyed the thrill of being pulled on a three-seater float that was attached behind the boat. When Dad turned and went over wakes, the boys would squeal in delight, flying in the air, sometimes staying on the float, sometimes diving midair into the lake. But they constantly crawled back up on the float and wanted more! That last summer, Alex and Anthony enjoyed one previous visit to Torch Lake with Luc. This time, the boys were too big to be pulled on a float behind the boat, but instead, they just hung out, 'chilling,' as teenagers do.

As he grew, so did that athletic prowess. By 12-13, he learned how to 'surf' behind the wake from the boat. He would let the rope pull him up from the water and then surf on the large wake the ship made, throwing the rope into the boat and surfing barefoot on the board, just standing and navigating like he was one with the water.

If given the choice, Luc always preferred that we went somewhere in Florida or to the coast of Lake Michigan – where there was water, or more precisely, waves big enough to break on the surf. He would grab his bodyboard and run to the biggest wave over and over and over... I remember how much he loved a good PB&J sandwich to refuel with on the beach. In Luc's last year, during Easter break, we took Alex and Anthony to Key Largo, Florida. The 'threesome' hung out, tried deep sea fishing, snorkeled, and ate many of dad's great hamburgers.

Friends Forever

Luc also had a musical side and started playing piano at 5 using the Suzuki Method. He had weekly piano lessons with a lovely woman who had taught for 50 years. *Twinkle, Twinkle Little Star* and *Clair de Lune* were his first pieces, and the method he used early on was to learn the right hand only initially. He had recitals twice a year and once even performed at a Sunday recital when he was 6, the day after Luc and I got stuck at a La Guardia airport hotel the night before.

We had a little roll-up electronic keyboard that he could practice on when away from the real piano at home. He was a trooper! He practiced on my electronic Clavinova piano, which was realistic with weighted keys. We then obtained a baby grand piano because his dad, Luc, and I played. Luc advanced to pieces that took several minutes to play, such as Pachelbel's Canon in D, which has a joyful, yet serene character often heard at weddings. He must have been nervous before each recital, but one would never have known it when he played. He was a natural.

When only 6 and 7, he attended summer Suzuki piano camps at George Fox University in Newberg, Oregon, with friends Mary and Henry, the children of my medical school girlfriend, Ellie. They had a blast running all over campus between practice and performances. Young but brave Luc played his right-handed piece on a 10-foot grand piano on the giant auditorium stage. The bench height and footrest were adjusted for his height, and after his short but perfect performance, he bowed to the audience in perfect Suzuki style. He would continue piano lessons and recitals for 8 more years.

By 14, school and sports occupied much of his time, and the piano lessons became challenging to fit into his already busy schedule. I recorded every recital, and if I couldn't get a good view of the stage, I always heard his long, elegant fingers moving across the keyboard. I am grateful that I will always have them to listen to.

Luc loved animals so much. He grew up with our many family pets as his constant companions. It started with the two young black labs plus two old cats. Then serendipitously, when Luc was 5, mom went to buy fish food for the goldfish we had recently won at a carnival, and surprise, there was a dog adoption event being held.

Luc and dad were up north at Torch Lake. Left to her own devices, I rescued a two-year-old chihuahua named Chico. As it turned out, dad wasn't a fan of this decision, but I couldn't resist–and Chico grew to be one of dad's favorites. Two years later, Chico and Luc rode together in the Beverly Hills, Michigan, Memorial Day parade with me, dad, and his sister in grandpa's old convertible Mustang. Sparty, the mascot for Michigan State, also rode along. What fun we had.

When Luc was 7, we searched for a kitten for him. We found a white kitten for Luc, and dad found a silver-striped kitten for himself. So, there we were, back to two cats, whom we called Snowy and Winter. Snowy was Luc's night-time story companion for quite a while. She was timid, and petting and holding her was challenging, so a few years later, we visited a cat adoption event to find the perfect kitten for Luc.

He held a few, then picked a beautiful, chill, longhaired-mahogany black kitten and named her Shadow. She was the perfect pet for Luc, and his cousin once told me that it made sense that Shadow was just as sweet and gentle as he was. She followed him around the house, looking for him when he was not home, and she slept with him every night. Luc was her person.

Me... & My Shadow...

In June 2020, we added 'pandemic pup' Henna, a 14-month-old 'Shepsky' (half German Shepard, half Siberian husky) to our family. As soon as she entered the house, she saw Luc and all 65 pounds of her bounded happily onto Luc's lap. Luc now had 'his' dog.

'All in' on the fun things, I recall one time in the summer of 2011 when Luc was 6, he enthusiastically participated in the Beverly Hills (Michigan) longest lemonade stand. The event made it into the Guinness World Records. He and dad built, painted, and served mom-made lemonade on a warm August day. The stand was light blue with white dog prints and bowls of water for all dogs that walked by and couldn't have lemonade.

He was just so much fun and often silly when he was young. As I recall, he was between 5 and 7 when he would run around the house making a cute pterodactyl sound (what he thought they sounded like), although otherwise, he was not really into dinosaurs. Once, when we went to the drugstore together, he saw all the advertisements for vitamins and thought this would be a good place for zombies to shop because they needed vitamins!

One time, when he was probably 5, we suddenly had to slow down to avoid a minor car fender-bumper accident while he was riding in the car with me. The next thing I knew, without prompting, Luc was in his booster seat belting, 'Nationwide is on your side!' He was always thinking and always clever!

As a little boy, his childhood friends came over to play and loved to go through a friendly neighbor's backyard to get to the Rouge River and explore the paths. They also climbed the neighbors' trees to see how high they could get. Mom and dad (mostly mom) drove Luc to meet friends at a nearby sledding hill in the winter. Over and over, they went up and slid down that snow-covered hill. Luc wore his snow ski helmet, as his mom suggested, and dad had hot cocoa ready when we came home. Our family seemed to function as a well-oiled team.

Ethan was Luc's best friend in middle school and was one year older. They were the same size physically and stuck like glue to each other until Ethan went to a different high school the year before Luc did. Unfortunately, that's when they drifted apart, but I always thought they would find each other again after high school.

Ethan shared a story with me about a sleepover when they were 12, where they snuck out at night and walked a block to go onto a nearby golf course.

According to Ethan, they took my big pink exercise ball and kicked it around in the dark on the green of the golf course. Stopping and ducking if they saw car lights coming on the nearby road. Eventually, they thought they might get caught and get in trouble, so they ran home with that big pink ball, stealthily entering the house undetected.

Stories like these are treasures now and should have been shared with me 'someday' by Luc, yet I am stuck in a space of duality now – grateful to hear them even though they also sting of what won't ever be.

These two friends, Ethan and Luc, met while playing in Birmingham House Hockey, and they played on the same team for years. Both boys learned how to ride bikes when they were 10 and 11, another challenge they conquered as friends. It seemed they lacked the motivation to do so because their parents drove them to most places. I became determined to get these kids on bikes, finding two used bikes for sale through a neighborhood online site. They had outgrown 'little kid' bikes, so I 'nudged' them onto the bigger bikes with rewards, and soon they were off on their own. There was no stopping them from there; they rode to each other's houses and went on biking adventures together regularly. I am sure Ethan has kept some stories just for himself, but I am grateful they had this time.

Learning how to bike wasn't just utilitarian; it also broadened Luc's horizons. When he met Alex, a close friend for the last 3 years of Luc's life, both were still too young to drive. They would go to Dodge Park in Sterling Heights, where Alex lived, and bike for hours, or sometimes Alex would come to Beverly Hills, where we lived, and go into Birmingham. We lived 30 minutes apart, but both parents would regularly toss the boys' bikes into our vehicles and drive to the other –just so they could ride together.

Once, I took Luc and his bicycle to Sterling Heights in our truck adorned with a sticker magnet that read, 'Please Be Patient, Student Driver,' as Luc had started driving lessons by now. When I backed out of Alex's driveway, the rear camera didn't work, and I backed into Alex's dad's car! Crushing the doors on the driver's side, and the windows shattered. Luc and Alex helped get the glass out of the street and car, and Alex's dad was mainly worried about his beloved fishing pole. Luc and Alex laughed over that, though I was mortified! Apparently, mom was actually the 'student driver' that day!

Luc began his video gaming phase at 5 with the Wii, playing primarily with the family. Bowling was his favorite, and he got so excited when anyone made a strike. He put all his little five-year-old body into swinging the Wii stick like a bowling ball, and I was worried he would throw the Wii stick right into the TV screen! He also played other games, especially Minecraft, on his iPad mini. His dad liked playing football and a few games, so we got an Xbox and went through many controllers.

Luc and his friends especially enjoyed building on Minecraft. Once, I heard many meows coming from the basement, and when I checked it out, I saw that they had created a large Minecraft farm with dozens of cats roaming happily around on the screen. When Luc got older, he wanted to build a gaming computer, and I am sure he could have, but he settled for an already-made one instead and made several additions.

Ethan and Luc also shared a YouTube channel called Ultimate Gamer. They would play their games, mainly Grand Theft Auto and Call of Duty, trying to hit trick shots, recording them, and commentating. Ethan said the channel never got too big, and its subscribers hit around one thousand. They loved watching YouTube and wanted to be lucky enough to call it their job.

family
is
EVERYTHING

Alex and Luc met while playing Fortnight, which came out before COVID-19, and then gamers played it all the time. Anthony became Luc's close friend through Alex. They became a 'threesome'. They played many games; Luc even showed Anthony how to make money playing Minecraft, says Anthony. The three of them enjoyed many video games and always tried new ones. Luc's dad still plays Battlefield with Luc's login, and Alex joins in from his Xbox. The car racing video game Forza was a favorite, and Luc's 'car' is still driving. Today, Alex can challenge the car to races, or they can just drive around the map together. That feels incredible to me.

When the pandemic of 2020 reared its ugly head during Luc's 8th-grade year, precautions lasted well into 2021 in our Michigan county. The shutdown was brutal for our family, and his sister had moved in the summer before, after finishing grad school. It was supposed to be for one year, but the pandemic made it difficult for her to move and find a roommate. To top it off, since I worked in a hospital, I still went to the hospital to work and tested positive for COVID-19 on the first day of the shutdown.

Now we were quarantined, dad lost his taste and smell, and Luc had a scratchy throat. We didn't 'stock up' ahead of time, and fortunately, Luc's K-8 school and our church, Our Lady Queen of Martyrs (OLQM), placed sundry items on our porch, along with meals. Luc took his classes on Zoom, and his 8th-grade graduation was in the school parking lot. Luc's confirmation was delayed until September, and only parents could attend, and all had a pew. The pandemic canceled the family summer trip to Europe (the first time for Luc) and his 8th-grade trip to Cedar Point Amusement Park.

Among 'the canceled' for the summer of 2020 was driver's education, and he had to wait until Spring 2021. That spring, he did get his wish to go to Florida for Easter break, and we took Alex, everyone wearing masks, on the airplane and at the Marriott. His first year in high school was on and off Zoom. Hockey practices and games were irregular; temperatures were taken, masks were required, and only parents could attend. Luc's debate class was early on, and wearing masks caused the facial expression portion to be omitted. There was not a homecoming or prom.

The excitement to attend his dad's alma mater, play hockey, learn new things, and form new friendships was markedly diminished. This is when our youth had to 'hang out' online, and Luc and his friends stayed in touch playing video games. On Thanksgiving that year, he thanked his mom because she worked at a children's hospital, helping sick kids and volunteering at an adult hospital during Covid 19. He also thanked his parents for supporting the family with love and protection.

Hockey buddy, good friend Cade had this to share:

"Luc was a kind soul and special person. When people ask about you, I tell them things I could never say about anyone else: you were truly one of a kind. As time goes by, I've thought about you a lot. I always carry you with me through each step of my day, whether that's in my heart or physically...I carry your photo in my wallet everywhere I go, and recently I got your name tattooed on me to keep your name alive and with me every day."

Luc worked as a camp counselor at our neighborhood gym the two summers before his 11th year of school started. Supervising young children through activities inside and outside of our large neighborhood gym. The first-year COVID precautions were still in full swing, and masks had to be worn by all camp participants and also all of the workers.

Luc was well-liked by his co-workers and the younger campers, even though he told us he often had to tell them to keep their hands to yourself, act nice, or time to board the bus for the field trip. This 'in charge' demeanor earned him a nickname among the camp kids, and they even (jokingly) replaced his name sticker with one that read 'Karen,' which Luc thought was funny.

In September 2021, Luc turned 16, and we got him his first used car - a 2015 Jeep Cherokee; his dad made sure it couldn't go too fast to protect him as much as we could from auto accidents. He loved the vehicle and went to his first and only homecoming for BRHS, taking a lovely exchange student from Austria. The other boys took 'friend girls' they went to middle school with; if they had 'real' girlfriends, they took them. His dad and I thought Luc having a vehicle was a time saver because now he could get to and from school and to all those hockey practices, sometimes giving another hockey player a ride. Looking back, after Luc was gone, I sadly realized I had missed a full year of driving him around and having mom/son conversations, even if brief, because of teenager awkwardness or earbuds.

Luc was very devoted to the family and loved them all very much. We enjoyed the backyard pool, snow skiing, Florida beaches, eating dad's great cooking, and just being together. His favorite restaurant was Kyoto's, a Japanese Hibachi restaurant. He loved how they cooked on a grill right in front of you. The food was great and was always a memorable bonding experience with friends and family.

A former nanny shared:

"Luc and my son, Daniel, were buddies when they were younger. If I could talk to Luc one more time, I'd let him know how loved and important he is, that he wasn't in this battle alone, and that I wish we had known more about his struggle. My son, Daniel, was going through much of the same. He had actually asked me if we could get back in touch with Luc just a month or two before Luc's passing, and I told Daniel that Luc was probably very busy. I regret that more than anyone will ever know. I didn't realize it then, but our boys may have needed one another, and I allowed our busy lives to get in the way of that."

We will never know why Luc took his own life. Looking back on his years here, we can point to events and wonder. When he was 9, his favorite uncle, Dan who was at our house often, died suddenly and unexpectedly. Less than a month later, another 'uncle,' a best friend of Luc's dad, died by suicide. He grew up close to both of them. Everyone was perplexed by the suicide of this second uncle because he seemed to have 'everything,' a great job, wife, kids, friends, and even a second house on a lake. Yet, now we know, often there are no apparent signs.

On the surface, to most - 'he looked OK.' Both of these deaths were very traumatic for Luc, and he cried audibly at both funeral services; everyone could hear his heartbroken sobs. He went to some child counseling afterward and seemed to move forward. A couple of years later, Luc went to counseling for his anxiety, finding one good counselor, who soon after took a different job. We found another, but he didn't bond well with that therapist. Soon, the pandemic was upon us, and everything changed. High school was fast approaching, and Luc seemed to be adjusting as best he could. I knew that I would only have Luc for the high school years, and then he would go away to college. I didn't realize then that only two years would be all we would get once high school started.

The experience of losing a child to suicide, with or without apparent indicators and reasons, causes unbearable deep pain for the parents. What could we have done? Are we at fault? Were there signs before the last month that we could have acted on? After he requested to change high schools two weeks after school started, we immediately became 'aware' that something serious was amiss. Immediately, we found a recommended adolescent psychologist. It just wasn't enough. Luc must have had his mind made up.

And while a person can't go back in time, as we all wonder about..we must go forward and follow our nudges to reach out to someone we haven't seen or heard from in a while. To check in, see how they are doing, get together, and let them know you are there for them and how loved they are. So often, a person goes through trials and tribulations alone, keeping a stiff upper lip and looking 'OK' to everyone. Living in a depression that is causing deep, deep pain, and they don't know a way out. Kindness, conversation, a solid hug, a caring touch, and loving eye contact might be the thing that makes them feel life can be negotiable after all, to not give up, and a way out could be possible.

Luc left such an impression on everyone he left behind. As evidenced by the multitude of quotes from friends, teachers, coaches, and family. Adults noticed him growing up as an outstanding young man. So loved and admired. Goofy and silly with a sly smile. Always making others feel comfortable. Such a solid moral character—such an old soul. A loving, caring person, always looking out for the little guy, especially those who looked left out. Noble and disapproving when schoolmates picked on each other or disrespected teachers.

Luc. Such a tremendous athlete but never a 'jock.' He swam like a fish, surfed behind a boat, snow skied like a professional, played lacrosse competitively, and moved so fast! Luc's #1 sport was hockey, and he excelled at being a sharp-eyed, quick goalie. Using the Suzuki method and playing the piano until he was 12... I sure did love going to those recitals.

Luc was kind, conscientious, gorgeous, handsome, perfect, and sometimes socially awkward and quiet. He loved the family's ongoing menagerie of pets, especially his cat Shadow. He was a camp counselor for young children, took lifeguard lessons, and was a budding photographer. Loving his two older sisters so, so much. Spending 17 years and 4 days of his life with me was such a gift. Dad and I couldn't have asked for a better son. Luc was a blessing, bringing everyone so much joy, and he was my miracle child.

Alexander David Mullins

June 16, 1995 - August 7, 2016

Alex

The Cheerful Boy Alexander & His Reluctant, Hopeful, Not-So-Good, Very Resilient Mom

An Essay by this Legacy Project's Creator on a Cheerful Boy, Resiliency, and Community After Suicide Loss

"The Cheerful Boy" is the title of a painting my son Alex created when he was in 3rd grade—the same year he painted *The (darn) Tree.'* I share *that* story in Volume 3. Since losing Alex, I've noticed that certain serendipitous moments in life seem to catch me off guard. Some are unmistakable and profound, while others reveal themselves over time. In spirit, Alex has a way of communicating things that I deeply need to understand, and this time, it was through another cherished piece of artwork from his childhood.

I've always felt that *'The Cheerful Boy'* held a special significance. Countless times, long before Alex died, I have found myself stopping to stare at it, lost in thought and emotion. I framed this painting alongside *'The Tree'* many, many years before Alex left us. Looking back, it feels as though I had an intuitive knowledge—a kind of deep, inner knowing that these two pieces would hold great importance, even if I couldn't possibly understand why at the time.

What made Alex so insightful and wise in 3rd grade? And why are so many poignant messages from that period of his life surfacing now, after his absence?

The timing is not lost on me—he was in his seventh year of life, a number that seems to echo throughout his life (& death). Maybe it was the years just before his sweet innocence faded and his connection to something deeper (across the veil) started to wane. I digress; that's a complex subject for another time. I feel there's something truly significant in this reflection, though - I'm on to something.

Since losing a child, I've had to navigate a landscape of grief that reshaped my thoughts, actions, and sense of being. In the early days, we grievers find ourselves without a navigation system; we have to do whatever it takes to survive. Then, once we realize the world is still turning, we face a choice: to give up or to learn, adapt, and grow. Early on, I was determined to find a way to do these things... to live again but figuring out how to do that felt elusive for quite some time.

Then, one day, even if only briefly, 'hope' appeared. Soon after, allowing 'hope' in for a wee bit longer each time, 'she' eventually introduced me to her unwavering partner-in-crime-- Resilience. They became a comforting presence in my life, though I won't deny that welcoming them was a struggle.

Resilience has emerged as one of the most profound lessons I've mastered since Alex's unexpected passing. Today, I wish to share a piece about resilience that I originally wrote for another audience, but it feels so relevant to share here. In the years following the heartbreaking loss of my 21-year-old son Alex to suicide on August 7, 2016, I've come to understand the true essence of resilience. I want to highlight why it matters so much, where to find it, and how it connects to Alex's theme of cheerfulness—at least from my perspective.

The 'How I Found Resiliency' Piece:

"Alex is dead, Mom." *These four words spilled out of my youngest son's mouth on a presumably typical Sunday in August of 2016—words that will forever ring in a chasmic hollow echo just beyond my comprehension.*

Only moments after telling my husband G.R. about the inexplicable 'off' feeling I had been having all morning, my 18-year-old son, Parker, got a call from a friend of his brother. That call put him standing in front of me on a tired spot of carpet in my bedroom, fighting to say those four words— words that completely decimated everything in their path.

I heard Parker when he spoke, but somehow, hearing it and comprehending it were very different things. It was not possible. Yet, it was. Life as our family knew it had ended in that moment; it ended with Alex's last breath.

Alex died by suicide while away at college, building his brilliant future life. There was no warning. He went from being a handsome, accomplished, talented, gregarious, and intelligent young man...to gone. He had many friends, big goals, and a lot of dreams. He bear-hugged me only eight days prior as he chimed, "I love you, Mom. I'll be home in a few weeks." It wasn't to be.

Yet somehow, when I awoke the day after, in what felt like a universal defiance, the whole world still went on...The moments, days, and weeks that followed are still a blur. My heart lay in shattered pieces all around me.

This was my reality? I was thrust into a world I no longer recognized. My reflection was one I no longer knew. I was utterly lost in a heavy grief fog inside a vast, bottomless abyss of guilt, shame, and all the complications that suicide leaves behind. I passed...and I had trouble finding anything that was explicitly supportive. It seemed proper resources were scarce after a loss by suicide.

By year three, I was 'limping' my way through the grief and trauma when 'it' happened. Out on the road - far, far from that dreaded spot of carpet in my bedroom where those four devastating words had been spoken, 'it' happened - I had a transient ischemic attack (a minor stroke). It turned out that my 'body was keeping the score' - even if I wasn't. It was scary stuff.

In fact, the stroke terrified me. This [loss of my son], it seemed, might actually kill me, too, if I didn't do something very different going forward. After years of somehow knowing this could destroy me and unsure if I even cared, I suddenly knew in my soul that I wanted to figure it out... but how, since the world seemed to be lacking in places for real help.

Let me fill in a few details. In the first year, albeit barely, I survived by doing 'my best with what I had.' In year two, as glimmers of hope emerged, my husband and I made a plan: find new joy and a new way to live. I felt like I was just wasting away in our newly 'empty nest' that was heavily coated in a thick blanket of traumatic loss. The plan was equal parts drastic and straightforward.

We sold two businesses, our home, and most of our possessions. In their place, we put a rolling behemoth we christened "Yolo" (= you only live once) in honor of Alex and set out—toward the horizon. Yolo was a 40-foot fancy-ish motor home; our tiny abode on wheels. Our mission: take a few years to simplify, breathe, and figure out what - and where - was next. In a bit of commingled clarity meets madness, we had stripped our lives down to the 'studs' so we could rebuild. We had zero clue, no 'blueprints,' and wielded not so much as a proverbial hammer to start the rebuilding; still, off we went.

Our approach was drastic by most standards, but it was what right, for us. Many factors converged at once; some were there before the loss. Nevertheless, the actual final catalyst was Alex's death, which left a sense of 'WTF are we waiting for?' in its wake and catapulted us to make those (massive) changes.

Over the next two years, we traveled far from the safety of our hometown in the Midwest. We traveled east, wandered south, and even headed west, looking in 'nooks and crannies' for that elusive joy. Alex's dog, Harper, was our constant companion who needed us as much as we needed her. We tried to relax and do 'fun things,' but we weren't quite hitting the mark - we were just skirting the edges. Like the saying "time heals all wounds," it seems time has no actual magical powers to heal trauma like this - time just passes. It's what we do with the time that matters.

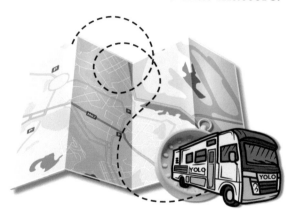

A few years ago, looking back at how hard my journey was during those first three years, I knew I had to do something for other moms like me. While roaming the country in search of something I couldn't truly define after my stroke (I called it 'joy' - but really, cheerfulness came first), I began the herculean task of picking up my leftover pieces. A 'seed' had been planted years ago but needed to be cultivated- brought out of dormancy.

That seed came two months into the loss of my son; the first time I was face-to-face, heart-to-heart, with another mom who had lost her child to suicide three years earlier. I knew the connection was precious and unique from when Tracy and I locked eyes. I knew it held a safety that no other place could.

Years later, that same seed was cultivated and bloomed into my heart's mission —to create a place of comfort, connection, and healing—specifically for grievers who have lost someone to suicide. "*The Leftover Pieces; Suicide Loss Conversations*" podcast came directly from that initial motivation. And I kept going from there - digging into education, certifications, and more - only wanting to be sure no other mom had to feel so lost, so alone, like I did those first few years. As a mother, it only made sense for me to work with other mothers from a place of shared understanding.

It all ended for me while looking into my youngest's eyes, right there on that single, innocent spot on the carpet where I heard the words that no parent can ever prepare for, let alone live with.

However, it began anew as I took hold, leaning into the support of other moms and I became a persistent, consistent champion in having meaningful conversations about suicide, mental health, trauma, and grief - for others, for myself.

The new life I have 'constructed' was not planned; it looks very different than I could have imagined, yet somehow, it works for us. As it turns out, dreams and purpose were still waiting to be found, maybe they look different than before, but they are still there. It was worth the work it took to get here. While nothing about this was easy, simple, or quick, anyone can survive, find hope, and move into a healing space just as I have. I know this is lonely, but you do not have to be alone. There is always hope for a brighter future.

I practiced resilience by cultivating a seed that bloomed into my heart's mission —creating a place of comfort, connection, and healing— just for grievers who have lost someone to suicide. The podcast came directly from that initial motivation. I kept going from there - digging into education, and certifications - wanting to be sure no other mom had to feel so lost, so alone, like I did those first few years. It only made sense for me to do direct work (aside from the podcast) with other mothers from a place of shared understanding. Things that I do now, like this project, courses, support communities, retreats and more came from that exact place.

I want every single devastated person who has lost someone to suicide to take away this message - "Find your people." This isn't just a trendy phrase; it's essential for healing. It's crucial to find and connect with others who are bereaved by the same relational suicide loss as you - and as soon as you possibly can. Moms need moms. If you are a sibling, seek sibling suicide loss support. Husbands or wives, find other spouses widowed by suicide. You get what I mean. Make no mind if it's online or in person; today, online community spaces allow for more choices when in-person options are slim. These people will become your lifeline, your guiding light, and your safe harbor... and I promise, you will be grateful they are there.

End Resiliency Piece

Indeed, this community of moms has given me so much more than I could ever offer them. Have I really "*sprung back into shape,*" as we often think of with resilience? Kind of. In less of a '*yep, that's the old me*' way and in more of a '*funhouse mirror reflection*' kind of way; I am here—*it's me* —and, yet it isn't. This transformation, as it seems, occurs best in the process of witnessing, nurturing, engaging with, and leaning into a community, our peers in grief.

Cheerful. I think Alex was cheerful - let's call it his inner "Tiggerness," if you will. When I think of the *Hundred Acre Wood* and its beloved characters, I see Alex as Tigger. While others around him seem weighed down by their struggles, loneliness, or sadness, Tigger stands out with his exuberance. Yet, we must ponder: Is Tigger genuinely happy, or is he simply 'bouncy and fun, fun, fun' as a way to conceal deeper emotions? Is Tigger's role, his purpose as he sees it, merely to uplift others, which is why he remains cheerful? But Tigger also has the hope of Eeyore, the matter-of-factness of Rabbit, the kindness of Piglet, and the resilience of Pooh. Tigger has his community - because together, we are all always better. Alex needed to reach out but may have been afraid to lay down the cheerfulness...

So, *how do we know* when cheerfulness falls short? We often wear cheerfulness as a mask, with a painted smile that hides our true feelings. On the other hand, joy (or happiness) comes from a much deeper place within us, illuminating our souls and shining through our eyes. They may seem alike initially, but look carefully, and you'll perceive the distinction. Look often and never be afraid to ask someone what they need.

I do want to say that it is okay if we wear a cheerful facade before experiencing true happiness. By letting hope in, this cheerfulness can evolve into something more profound. If we allow it, hope--borrowing courage from within--can light our way forward. To overcome adversity, it helps to build resilience, and when nurtured by a community of survivors, it can lead us down a winding path toward true happiness.

When I first saw Alex's painting's title, "*The Cheerful Boy,*" I was taken aback. It felt like such an adult word for someone so young. Why not 'The Happy Boy,' Alex? Cheerful means: *bringing happiness just by its nature or appearance, which is more of an outside expression, not an inner one*' So, being cheerful is not the same as *being* happy. Do you see the difference?

According to the Oxford Dictionary, "cheerful" means *showing* happiness or optimism, while "happy" refers to the deeper *feelings* of pleasure or contentment. The distinction lies in the context that cheerfulness pertains to our interactions with others, while happiness reflects our inner emotional state. Resilience doesn't do the job alone, though. If we stop with just resilience, we can fall short but never fear. Resilience has friends like Hope, Courage, Tenacity; all the helpful 'besties' we need to start to rebuild after a traumatic loss.

> Robin Williams once said, "I think the saddest people always try their hardest to make others happy because they know what it's like to feel absolutely worthless, and they don't want anyone else to feel that way."

At just 7 years old, how did 'artist Alex' even realize that the cheerful face he showed the world wasn't a complete reflection of his inner feelings? Cognitively, I am certain he didn't and it fascinates me what intuition can do--where are those 'inner voices' based?

Alex always came across as an old soul. He was kind, funny, and wise in a way that could be both inspiring sometimes frustrating, often comedic. His wisdom surpassed his years. He embraced life and loved adventure. He loved his family, his friends, and all animals. He was there for everyone and always the life of the room. Alex typically seemed *so* happy. *And* he died by suicide. Masks. Fear. Cheerfulness.

How Alex died will never fully make sense, but we must find hope in the fact that his life was so much more than just those few moments when he left. Every second he lived— nearly two-hundred and sixty-three *million* of them to be exact—deserve attention and acknowledgment. Each moment is a part of who he was and still is. It is his legacy. Thus, the work I do with The Leftover Pieces Community is part of that Legacy as well.

Even now, Alex continues to teach me from *beyond*. I am learning to listen and grow; he wants me to continue striving for true happiness, not just a cheerful facade. That, is the lesson of my cheerful boy. Most of the time, I do quite well at the 'assignment', *and* I miss him single every day

My son coaxes me to own my resilience and dive courageously into living fully. It's in the diving that the changes happen. He knows my perspective has shifted and inspires me daily to navigate this unexpected path. Alex deserves to be remembered, honored, and talked about. Reluctance conquered by resilience has paved the way forward, with hope lighting the way, reminding me that the significance of his life—the countless little and big moments that shaped who he was all still matter.

Thank you for taking the time to read part of his story and indulge me sharing parts of mine since he left us. May it inspire you to remember cheerful masks are okay and fear is normal, but it's by letting in hope, and those who understand, that you will find resiliency waiting for you to take it from there. *Thanks for the reminder, Alex!*

With Heartfelt Gratitude,
Shattered, Reluctant, Hopeful, Not-So-Good,
Very Resilient 'ol Me (Melissa)

Love, & Legacy Remain

This is that 'spot' -- the place in a book where *everything* you have read gets 'wrapped up' and tied with a neat 'bow.' At least that's the typical model, right? This, however, is different from a usual book. In this collection, after these genuinely incredible stories from lives cut way (*way*) too short, a 'conclusion' lands differently.

As a student of ancient philosophy, I know that the concept of *memento mori* is never far from my mind. I even carry a talisman as a reminder that life is short *&* to live fully. *Memento mori* is a Latin phrase meaning "remember you must die." The notion of 'remembering death' appears throughout Europe, and other cultures have traditions that approach the same concept in unique ways. In speaking of legacy, it is remembering one's life with value *after* the life has ended. Stoics focus on living a life of virtue, and whether it has any (real) value after we are gone is, well, debatable. This idea poses a tricky, slicker-y spot for a grieving mom. I have spent much time in quiet, tear-filled moments of contemplation due to this quandary.

But *if* life has no value beyond life, as the stoics may have thought, then why do we study the lives of those gone— searching for meaning and answers to the questions we seek answers to during our lives?

Acclaimed writer and (modern) stoic Ryan Holiday put it like this in his book The Obstacle Is the Way (2014), summarizing the Stoic approach to legacy by saying, "*The impediment to action advances action. What stands in the way becomes the way.*"

Stoics prioritize living virtuously in the present rather than seeking enduring recognition or external validation. Okay. I get that, but that doesn't mean those who loved us can't benefit from our story --from our triumphs and strife, our jubilations and our torments. What about the benefit to those who didn't know (let alone love) us? They can benefit from knowing. Actually, I know they can. This is why we even know who the Stoics were: it's why we know who Abraham Lincoln, MLK, RBG, and even Walt Disney were.

Because legacy matters. Luc, Skyler, and Alex matter. Your loved ones matter. Their mark was made, and they deserve a spotlight.

The great poet May Angelou once said, "*If you are going to live, leave a legacy. Make a mark on the world that can't be erased.*"

Suicide is only one action - it is *not* a legacy. Suicide is not who they were *or* how they lived. It has nothing to do with their life except one moment among many. It is, it was, simply a singular act -- one that is not about dying but so much more about escaping human struggle in a moment - escape from an inflicted mind is complex. *While it may be definitive, it's not definite.* Our absolute power lies in the millions of tiny moments that make up a whole life, not a single moment that brings death.

"*Death is not the opposite of life, but a part of it,*" H. Murakami.

And then there's this—it's so true. So, while embracing death can feel impossible, knowing that we can (learn to) fold it in as a moment-- seeing it as a minor stroke on a large canvas filled with all of the colors of life's countless moments, somehow takes on a new perspective—*one that can bring comfort and ease the burden we often carry.*

This book, these stories of the incredible lives these young men lived, the powerful stories of their lives told by those who know firsthand that their impact created ripples that should continue that others can still benefit from. Legacy allows those left behind, whether they knew us in life or not, to be affected and to know them, even a little bit.

This—all of this that you just read is why this book intends to be read, reread, and passed on so that someone else may do the same. It is why those who loved them will read it to remember and feel close to them again, and it is why those who didn't know them will feel as if they did and take that into their lives so that it can have a ripple effect in their lives. It matters this legacy thing. It truly does.

So, while the duality is sharp, I wish I had never (ever) had this reason to know Suzanne and Sharon, and indeed the same for Skyler and Luc. I am also eternally grateful that they are a part of the rest of my life, and I am thankful that Alex knows these incredible souls beyond this life. These things help a mom's heart.

Since its inception in early 2023, this legacy project has been completed five times (with this publishing) and has been helpful to all of the moms who have participated. I know it continues to help me, and I will continue doing it as long as there are moms desiring this outcome.

This project is significant to me. It provides an opportunity to help mothers who are trying to heal from their grief and learn to live successfully after loss. If you are a bereaved mother reading this or know someone who is, please feel free to reach out. As I move toward a singular start date every year in 2025 (not the 2-3 times in previous years), getting on the project list as soon as possible is vital. Let's come together to share your child's story with the world.

Stories have always been a critical part of how we communicate. Their true strength comes from sharing them with others. Please read these stories often and share them with anyone interested in learning about these young men. I am very proud of what these moms have achieved in this book. Take their stories forward. Remember their names, and share their stories with anyone who will listen.

By sharing memories and stories, we can connect with others, inspire change, and positively impact the world. Let's not keep these stories to ourselves; let's share them to help create a better today and a brighter tomorrow.

"*No matter what happens in life, be good to people. Being good to people is a wonderful legacy to leave behind.*"
– T Swift.

Warmly, Melissa

Learn More About the Project HERE:

About the Moms

Suzanne Little

Skyler's Mom

Suzanne always wanted to be a mom. Even as a child, she pretended to have her "babies" to care for. So, needless to say, she was elated to become a mom several times over—eight times, to be precise. Her love for her children is boundless, and like many moms, she has spent her life supporting them and helping them grow and develop into the people they want to be.

Suzanne and her husband, Skip, built a beautiful family and shared countless adventures with their children. From cruises to Disney, Rome, and beyond, these experiences are now cherished memories. Despite the recent losses of Skip and her oldest son, Skyler, Suzanne is determined to keep their spirits alive. She continues to find ways to honor them through her daily actions and how she lives her life.

When she's not working, Suzanne indulges in her hobbies. She loves to travel, bake, and spend time with her four-legged babies. An avid reader, she also enjoys solving puzzles of all kinds. Her passion for college football, especially for her beloved Georgia Bulldogs, has been a constant since childhood. Go, Dawgs!

Suzanne writes in memory of Skyler

Dr. Sharon Kemper

Lucs' Mom

Dr. Sharon Kemper is a wife to Mark, mother to son Luc, stepmother to two grown girls, Lanie and Cece, and 'Mimi' to Lanie and Tim's two little girls, Lucy and Mady. Luc's cat, Shadow, and dog, Henna, are also cherished family members.

Born in Buffalo, New York, and traveling across the United States three times as a child, Dr. Kemper finally landed in Houston, Texas, where she graduated from high school—encouraged to go into cosmetology by the high school counselor as none of her family had ever gone on to college. After only one year as a hairdresser, Sharon decided to attend college. Starting first in community college while working part-time, taking student loans, and having military assistance (a benefit from her deceased father), she made it-- to medical school. Moving to Michigan, Dr. Kemper completed residency/fellowship and has been practicing as a pediatric anesthesiologist there for 25 years.

Not (originally) planning to stay in Michigan, she met her husband Mark, and the rest, as they say, is history. They have now been married for twenty-two years. Eager to become parents, beautiful baby Luc came into their life three years after they wed. For the first four years of Luc's life, she worked less to soak up and love him as much as possible. Besides being Luc's mom and a doctor, she has always enjoyed snow-skiing in Michigan and out-west with their family of five. Their house and family pool always seemed to be the gathering place for friends and large extended family. Michigan summers have the best weather, allowing seventeen treasured summers together as a family.

She writes in memory of her son Luc.

Melissa Bottorff-Arey

Alex's Mom

Melissa Bottorff-Arey is a wife, mother of three, and grandma to four incredible 'littles' (and her grand-pup Harper, Alex's dog, who lives with them). She married her college sweetheart after spending 20 years apart - making for a sweet 'love-for-the-ages-come-back-together' story with her husband, Garrison (mostly known as G.R. friends and family).

After achieving her dream career, this former Professional Chef retired her whisk and briefly worked alongside her husband, managing his home inspection business. However, after life shattered, she pivoted. Less of a choice and more of a calling; these roles came about after the unexpected death of her 21-year-old son ... making a choice (eventually) to put the shattered pieces of her heart back together; she now puts her whole heart into helping grieving moms like herself do the same.

In the winter of 2020, amidst a global lockdown, Melissa turned her pain and 'gift of gab' into a powerful weekly podcast where you will hear her have hard but meaningful conversations with other loss survivors. As a published author of multiple suicide loss guides and journals, she has been invited to speak on stages both locally and internationally. Trained as a Master Grief Coach, she now also leads support communities, teaches courses in trauma healing, leads legacy projects such as this compilation book, and even hosts healing retreats for moms in Puerto Rico multiple times a year.

Melissa thinks you needn't force a hobby when you have a passion for it. Still, she can sometimes be spotted pouring beeswax candles and caring for many plants. She can even be found in the kitchen chopping, dicing, and sautéing alongside G.R.- but now, just for the sheer love of it!

Melissa writes, leads and serves others in memory of Alex

About The Leftover Pieces

About The Leftover Pieces

♥

The Podcasts, Resources & A Community

The (OG) Podcast - November 2020 - present
"The Leftover Pieces; Suicide Loss Conversations" (for ALL survivors)

As she sees it, Melissa became a podcast listener by circumstance and a podcast creator, producer, and host by necessity. In the throes of the devastating loss of her 21-year-old son, Alex, by suicide, Melissa found reading grief books difficult in the early days. She thinks reading eluded her because the heavy 'brain fog' from the trauma of her loss made concentrating and absorbing more than a few sentences at a time impossible. Enter podcasts. She found several that entertained - even distracted her - and a few helped, but not enough. No one was tackling the topic of suicide grief, and loss specifically. So, one day, a few years in, the idea came - "I will just create what I need. I can do this." In just under a year, "The Leftover Pieces; Suicide Loss Conversations" Podcast went from an idea to social media, with the first episodes released in November 2020. Melissa believes strongly in the power of podcasting as both a resource and a powerful connection point for grievers. She also sees it as a specific and practical way to advocate, bring awareness and collaborate with others sharing the same mission on a global scale.

Find this Podcast HERE:

About The Leftover Pieces

♥

The Podcast, Resources & A Community

The (Second) Podcast - December 2025 - present
"Let's <u>Really</u> Talk About Suicide; Somewhere Between Complicated & Controversial" (for ALL survivors)

This podcast delves deep into the pressing and often sensitive issues surrounding the suicide crisis, particularly its impact on young people over the last decade. With a rotating co-host format, you can expect engaging conversations on a wide variety of topics, from bullying to social media, gaming to legislation, LGBTQ+ challenges to toxic leadership in the military, mental health to substance use and addiction, contagion to coercion, and more. The co-hosts bring various perspectives and knowledge from personal, lived experiences, education, and relevant backgrounds. Buckle up—we have so much to say!

[Please NOTE: This podcast is for only relational, informational, and entertainment purposes. It candidly and openly discusses sensitive and sometimes activating topics. There will be in-depth conversations that may be activating to those who live with mental illness or have survived a suicide loss. There is the possibility of detailed mention of suicide, murder, rape, and the like. Be guided and care for yourself accordingly. Melissa is not a doctor or licensed therapist, and while her co-hosts come from varying backgrounds, nothing on this podcast should be taken in place of, or as, medical/mental health advice or recommendations.]

Find this Podcast HERE:

The Resources *(for ALL survivors)*

Resources for You; Help Along the Way

Here you will find resources that may help you find the support you need and connect you to other suicide loss grievers and the communities where they connect. You will also find podcasts, apps & media to interact with. My recommended reading list includes books, journals & cards. I've also provided a list of professionals offering support, healing & coaching, and other beneficial national organizations. We cannot 'fix' or 'get over' this, but we can learn to live successfully alongside it, & filling our toolbox is a vital step. This page can help.

Find this page HERE:

The Community *(for child loss or sibling loss)*

Healing You; Finding Support

Are you a mom who has lost a child to suicide? Do you want to learn how to grow forward and belong to a community that really 'gets it'...? Then these (Online Private Zoom) support groups, courses (& more) are specifically designed for you! Let's pick up the pieces together. Groups will be led by Melissa and/or a qualified peer-leader. See the Calendar on this page for the current schedule.

Find this page HERE:

The Retreats
Empowered Healing - *(for moms after child loss)*

These retreats, the culmination of years of dreams and wishes, are a unique and exclusive offering. The first one, hosted in July 2024, was a testament to the power of hope and healing. They provide a one-of-a-kind, curated, and immersive experience exclusively for mothers who have lost a child to suicide--destined to be a part of The Leftover Pieces' world of hope and healing, where mothers who understand each other's pain and journey come together.

The ultimate goal of these retreats is to leave you feeling empowered and connected - to your soul, nature, and new mom friends you can't imagine not knowing as you move forward. It's about finding hope and inspiration amid loss, and we are here to guide you on this journey. Being surrounded by understanding and support allows you to open up and heal. You will leave the retreat feeling stronger, more connected, and with a renewed sense of hope.

Find My Home page HERE:
(& then navigate to the current Retreat Page)

The Legacy Project *(for moms)*

Discovering You; Remember Your Child

Do you want to be sure your child is remembered? This is one of the top needs we moms feel after losing our child. As a part of the Legacy Project, you can experience natural personal healing and have a permanent legacy for your child - a whole chapter about your child (written by you) in an exceptional published compilation book (just like this one).

When this project first went from dream to planning, I won't lie; I was worried if I would get it 'right.' Then the first session started and the rest, as they say, is history!

Having now had the honor of guiding & walking alongside many moms as they heal, write, & remember, I can say "Yes!" This project has actually exceeded my expectations & lived up to all dreams I had for it. Please consider joining us - & you do not have to be a writer to author their story - that's why we do this together. Check the page on my website for the current waitlist for an opportunity to participate in an upcoming project.

Learn More HERE:

theleftoverpieces.com

Made in the USA
Columbia, SC
06 January 2025

49354889R00082